Original title:
Pots and Promises

Copyright © 2025 Creative Arts Management OÜ
All rights reserved.

Author: Sophia Kingsley
ISBN HARDBACK: 978-1-80581-851-9
ISBN PAPERBACK: 978-1-80581-378-1
ISBN EBOOK: 978-1-80581-851-9

Resilience in the Grain

In a kitchen, things go wrong,
A spatula sings a silly song.
Flour flies like a wild parade,
While the chef's plans begin to fade.

Eggs roll out in a daring dance,
Bacon strips take a bold advance.
But chaos thrives in buttery bliss,
With every stumble, there's a twist!

The skillet sizzles, oh what joy,
As veggies play their playful ploy.
A spoon takes a leap, reaches the sky,
While the timer beeps, oh me, oh my!

Yet, in this mess, we learn to laugh,
As burnt bread gains a second draft.
With every flop, a lesson found,
In every crumb, a joy unbound!

The Art of Holding

A bowl that wobbles seems to grin,
Its rim is wide but holds me in.
With every twist, it starts to sway,
"Please don't drop me!" it seems to say.

I tried to stack it, what a flair!
One slipped and landed in my hair.
It laughed with glee, a clumsy jest,
Now I wear it, my new dessert.

Under the Glaze

A mug that's chipped, but oh so bright,
Holds tales of tea on winter nights.
It spills my secrets, not a care,
While I sip slowly, lost in air.

The colors run—a riotous show,
Was that green tea or jade? Who knows!
It bubbles softly, keeps me warm,
A quirky friend in ceramic form.

Charred Commitments

A dish that's blackened, looks so bold,
"Burn me again, I'm just too gold!"
The leftovers cling, a sticky mess,
In its cracked heart, I find finesse.

With every crack, a laugh erupts,
I tell my friends, "It's just how it fluffs!"
They roll their eyes, I wave my hand,
"Each charred embrace is love so grand."

Sculpted Futures

A statue formed from playful clay,
With goofy eyes that seem to sway.
It plans my lunch, I swear it said,
"Let's shape up folks—bring on the bread!"

A pinch of hope, a dash of cheer,
It dreams of feasts throughout the year.
With every mold, we laugh and play,
A future built in the quirkiest way.

Imprints of Tomorrow

With silly hands we shape our dreams,
A dented jug, or so it seems.
We'll bake our hopes, they'll rise and swell,
In mismatched cups, we cast our spell.

Each crack a giggle, each chip a jest,
In clay, we find our very best.
A tapestry of laughter spun,
In every dish, the joy won't run.

Glazed Reflections

A lid that wobbles, a bowl that drips,
We toast our quirks on clumsy trips.
The glaze is bright, but oh so wrong,
Our kitchens dance to a silly song.

With colors splattered like jumbled glee,
Mistakes become our recipe.
Each awkward angle, a story told,
In every hue, our hearts unfold.

Resilient Shapes

A mug that laughs when it spills its tea,
Says, 'Oops, that's just part of me!'
In twisted forms, we find some grace,
A quirky dance we all embrace.

No perfect curves in this merry land,
Just pots with quirks, we understand.
They wobble and roll, but who can frown?
In the clink of clay, we wear our crown.

Love's Fired Essence

In a kiln of quirks, our hearts ignite,
With laughter mixed in, oh what a sight!
The spatters of love, they warm the space,
In every corner, a funny face.

As embers glow, we toast our art,
Crafting clumsy vessels that warm the heart.
In each crooked curve, there's beauty found,
In our merry chaos, we gather round.

Serendipity in Saucers

In a cupboard stacked with dreams,
The saucers giggle, or so it seems.
They've seen antics of tea with glee,
Spinning stories, just you and me.

Cups do waltz, while spoons align,
Chasing crumbs like playful swine.
A saucer slips and takes a bow,
As laughter stirs the teapot's vow.

The sugar packet, winking bright,
Jumps in dance, such a silly sight.
Each spill of cream, a canvas bold,
Of laughter shared, as stories unfold.

Oh, the clinks and clatters, a lively score,
In this cabinet, we find much more.
With every sip, a promise brewed,
In sweet chaos, joy's never subdued.

The Bond of the Artisan

An artist's hands, so clay-stained bright,
Crafting shapes with a playful might.
"Oh dear, that cup is not quite round!"
It wobbles, then rolls, not making a sound.

The wheel spins fast, with laughter's breeze,
As pottery dreams come with such ease.
A mug waves hello, a bowl spins proud,
In this realm of fun, so alive and loud.

Each crack and fold tells tales most grand,
Of mishaps faced and stones unplanned.
With kiln's warmth, there's a fiery cheer,
For every mishap brings joy near.

Oh, bond of craft, let humor reign,
In every splash, laughter's sweet gain.
For in this clay, so soft yet tough,
We find a friendship, joyful and rough.

Breath of the Kiln

In the heat of a fiery lair,
The characters dance, with flair to spare.
"Is that a teapot or a chicken?" we jest,
With every glaze, they quirkily quest.

The oven whirs, a dragon's breath,
With bubbly laughs, they tease at death.
One vase sways, another might roll,
As art takes life, and we lose control.

The terracotta smiles, wild and bright,
Pots share secrets in the night.
Each crackling sound, a joke divine,
Creating bonds through the sparkling line.

So let's toast to this playful heat,
Where pottery dreams and laughter meet.
In every flaw, a giggling thrill,
For artistry lives in every hill.

Patterns of Pledged Hearts

In a workshop bustling, hearts collide,
With clay and laughter, side by side.
A mug says, "I'm not full, feel free!"
As they chat about love over a cup of tea.

Each pattern drawn, a quirky glance,
Hearts entwined in a joyful dance.
"Oops, that's an elephant, but wait! Oh dear,"
Mocked by a spoon that grins ear to ear.

With every spin, they seem to weave,
Stories of love, yet hard to believe.
A plate cracks under all the cheer,
As promises made turn crystal clear.

So here's to the shapes that find their way,
In this merry clay and playful play.
With every heart, a story starts,
In the world of laughter, we pledge our hearts.

Scent of the Kiln

In the corner sits a vessel,
With a handle like a noodle,
It winks at me in daylight,
Like it's part of some big riddle.

Once a mug, now a planter,
Filled with dirt, not tea or coffee,
I swear it whispered, 'Water me!'
But now it's just a joke of folly.

Reflections in Earth and Fire

A bowl that dreams of yummy dips,
Yet catches dust like a great sage,
I scoop out snacks and take a sip,
But it just smiles, what a cage!

A plate that sings of grand feasts,
But holds only crumbs and regrets,
I load it heavy with my fests,
It laughs, oh how it offsets!

Voices of the Silent

A teapot croaks with boiling glee,
'Fill me up!' I hear it shout,
But every time, I spill my tea,
It chuckles, 'You look like a lout!'

A sugar bowl, sweet as can be,
Whispers secrets in the night,
'Less is more!' it vows to me,
But my coffee says, 'Just one bite!'

Imbued with Promises

A clay cup dances on the shelf,
I see it laugh but hear it thud,
Promises of warmth, oh how it swells,
Yet spills my coffee like a flood.

Mismatched spoons rattle in their galas,
Each claims to stir the perfect blend,
Yet with every clink, they plan a tale,
Of bravado, chaos—a grand pretend!

The Kiln's Embrace

In the kiln where dreams do bake,
Mugs and bowls for goodness' sake.
Fire's dance, a snicker and spin,
   Hoping nothing cracks within.

Clay rebels, it wiggles a lot,
I swear it's got a playful plot.
Laughter bubbles, the glazes bloom,
   Will my vase escape its doom?

Firing up with a cheeky grin,
The pots are plotting, where to begin?
Spinning tales like a mischievous sprite,
   Oh, what adventures in the night!

So let's toast with our cups in hand,
To the chaos we can't quite understand.
With each chip, a memory plays,
In the kiln where we blaze our stay.

Secrets in the Glaze

Dipping brushes, secrets unfold,
Colors hidden, a tale to be told.
A splash of fun, a wink from the hue,
Crafting mischief, a playful crew.

Glaze that slips, a giggle escapes,
It's not just art, it's shaping landscapes.
With every coat, a story grows,
Will it shine bright or wear some woes?

Patterns mingle, like a dance of delight,
Underneath it all, they plot through the night.
Whispers of whimsy, bubbling with cheer,
Who knew painting could draw us near?

Each pot a misfit, unique in style,
Together they jest, with a cheeky smile.
In every crack, a laugh's embrace,
Unveiling tales in the silly space.

Earthen Echoes

From the ground, chaos arose,
Lumpy creations, how could this pose?
Echoes of laughter, as clay meets the wheel,
Surprising shapes that make you squeal.

Each bump and ridge, a friend gone wild,
Designing dreams, just like a child.
Mold it, shape it, but beware the flare,
It might just giggle and give you a scare!

When it dries, will it behave,
Or show you its wild side, funny and brave?
Take a peek, I dare you to see,
What truths are trapped under the debris!

So here's to the mess, the laughs all around,
In the fun of creation, joy can be found.
Embrace the echoes of earth's merry song,
For in the wild, we truly belong.

Crafted Connections

Hands in clay, they mold and squish,
Creating bonds, like an odd little fish.
One part silly, one part finesse,
Together they laugh at the glorious mess.

A pinch of joy, a dash of grace,
Stirring up friendships in this crazy place.
With mugs that chat and plates that tease,
Each crafted piece is sure to please.

Join the circle, spin the wheel,
Laughter echoes with every feel.
From weirdly shaped to a work of art,
Each connection forms a loving heart.

So lift your cup, share a grin,
In the joy of crafting, let the fun begin.
We're all just clay, being shaped anew,
In this playful dance, we find our crew.

Raw within the Refined

In kitchens where chaos meets clatter,
The chef finds joy in the splatter.
A bowl's embrace, a spoon's slight dance,
Mistakes inspire a recipe's romance.

On countertops, the veggies fume,
Mixed with laughter, they find their groove.
A sprinkle here, a giggle there,
Culinary chaos fills the air.

With each stir, the flavors collide,
A dash of humor, a pinch of pride.
What's behind the door of delight?
Soufflés rise with comedic heights.

In the kitchen, don't fear the mess,
Embrace the chaos, it's pure finesse.
For every flop, a tale unfolds,
In laughter's embrace, true art beholds.

The Color of Commitment

In a world painted bright, oh what a sight,
Colors clash and merge in joyful delight.
With brushes in hand, we create our fate,
Each splash tells a story, we can't wait.

A canvas of dreams, where we all reside,
Mixed up together, we take it in stride.
A hue of laughter, a stroke of cheer,
Brushes entwined, in the fun we steer.

The palette's sometimes a wild mess,
Where strokes of love can cause distress.
But in the chaos, we find our claim,
For painted moments, we're never the same.

Drawing our hearts with colors so bright,
In laughter and joy, we sip from the light.
A masterpiece formed through friendship's art,
Together we color the joy in our heart.

Formations of the Soul

From clay so soft, we shape our dreams,
With every twist, laughter always beams.
The wheel spins swiftly, a fun little ride,
As characters form and secrets abide.

With hands all messy and giggles so free,
We mold our stories, you and me.
Each crack and flaw tells a tale untold,
In shapes so funny, our hearts unfold.

As creations wobble, we catch our breath,
In each quirky curve, we find no death.
For the art we shape, with charm and spice,
Embraces the glories of imperfection's slice.

So let's roll in the dirt and embrace the joke,
Together we'll spin, until our hearts soak.
With laughter as glue, in this whimsical fold,
Art comes alive in the stories we mold.

The Heart of the Hearth

Around the fire, our stories ignite,
Flames of laughter blaze through the night.
With marshmallows roasting, we always tease,
As silly tales dance in the evening breeze.

The pot on the stove begins to bubble,
With secrets and giggles, oh what a trouble!
Stirring the broth of memories grand,
Each ladle reveals how we all understand.

A toast to the warmth in our cozy space,
Where humor and love find their embrace.
In the glow of the embers, we sip and share,
The heart of a home is found everywhere.

So gather around, let the stories flow,
In this heart of warmth, let the laughter grow.
For every memory brewed in the pot,
Is a bond that's formed, and can't be bought.

Embracing Imperfections

With wobbly cups, I serve my tea,
A splash of color, wild and free.
Each crack a story, a laughter shared,
In every stumble, joy is bared.

Oh, the saucers tilt, they dance divine,
A symphony of clinks, like vintage wine.
With every drip on tablecloth,
I wear my flaws, and laugh a lot.

So raise your mugs, let cheer arise,
In chaos found, true beauty lies.
For it's the fun in spilled delight,
That makes our evenings truly bright.

Wistful Whirls

In the cupboard, they spin around,
Chipped and cheerful, laughter found.
A whimsical dance, they twirl and sway,
Until they tumble, come what may.

A mug with ears, a bowl with legs,
Their wailing tunes, like worn-out begs.
Each spin a tale, each crack a song,
In splendid quirks, we all belong.

So join the ruckus, don't hold back,
In silly glances, no joy we lack.
For as we whirl and spin about,
Life's a laugh—let's scream and shout!

Touched by Warmth

With cozy mugs in friendly clutches,
We sip our drinks, exchanging hunches.
As steam curls up with tales so bright,
Each moment's warmth a pure delight.

The kettle hums a merry tune,
To serve us joy from late to noon.
A sprinkle here, a dash of that,
Every sip in giggles sat.

So slosh it wide, don't be precise,
In bubbling laughter, life's a slice.
From clinks of glass to hearty cheers,
In shared warmth, we conquer fears.

Echoes of Creation

In rippling glazes, colors clash,
An artist's dream, a playful splash.
With visions bright and wild designs,
From crafty hands, pure magic shines.

The laughter echoes through the clay,
Creating treasures, come what may.
Each piece a whisper of love and cheer,
In every curve, our hearts are near.

So throw the paint, let chaos reign,
From every mishap, we'll entertain.
With whimsy crafted, let spirits fly,
In the art of fun, we'll reach the sky.

Shadows of Covenant

In the garden where gnomes dance,
A ceramic frog wore a jaunty stance.
Each chip and crack tells a sly joke,
While daisies giggle beneath the oak.

A whimsical pot promises growth,
With flowers sprouting—a leafy oath.
But squirrels sneak in with a playful scam,
Stealing the seeds—oh, what a jam!

As shadows plot on a sunny day,
A faded smile just won't decay.
With laughter stitched in the rusty seams,
The secrets bloom in childish dreams.

When the rain falls and puddles form,
Even the clay can weather a storm.
For in this dance of soil and jest,
We plant our hopes—it's for the best!

Embers of Commitment

A kettle whistles the tune of fate,
While squirrels plot and conspirate.
With each bubbling laugh on the stove,
We share our tales, our secrets wove.

The teapot's dance is quite absurd,
As it twirls like a joyful bird.
And every sip brings a hearty grin,
In this merry chaos, we all win.

While crumbs linger on the table's edge,
There's warmth wrapped tightly in this pledge.
With flavors bold and stories grand,
Life's greatest feasts are close at hand.

The fire-tongue flickers, a playful spark,
As memories dance in the fading dark.
In these moments where laughter glows,
The sweetest embers nobody knows.

Rustic Recollections

With laughter painted on the walls,
And memories echoing in the halls,
Old spoons and forks recall the fun,
Where meals turned mundane into a run.

A wooden bowl holds tales so bright,
Of family feasts deep into the night.
With sticky hands and laughter loud,
In simple joys, we feel so proud.

The dust of time adds a misty hue,
To recipes shared between me and you.
Each taste a story, each bite a song,
In every flavor, where we belong.

Together we stir the pots of cheer,
With every whisk, our hearts draw near.
In a rustic dance where we all sway,
Cooking up dreams in a funny way!

Shaping the Future

Crafting tomorrow with a silly grin,
As spatulas spin in a whimsical spin.
With flour clouds marking our face,
We race to make our favorite place.

A sprinkle of laughter, a dash of fun,
Creating a feast where all can run.
With bowls that wobble and lids that fly,
We whip up futures that leap sky-high.

In our kitchen, chaos reigns supreme,
Where every mishap fuels a dream.
And as the batter takes its flight,
We bake our hopes into the night.

For shaping the future is a messy art,
Filled with giggles and a happy heart.
Together we rise, just like the bread,
In this dance of joy, we're always fed!

Nestled in the Vessel

In the corner sat a bowl,
With an orange peel's lost soul.
Oh, the tales it could regale,
If only it could tell a tale!

A mug that danced with morning cheer,
Tipped a wink, said, "Drink, don't fear!"
While spoons conspired in the night,
Stirring pots of pure delight.

A kettle sings a bubbling tune,
Whistling freely, over the moon.
Lid askew, it spills its dreams,
In a kitchen filled with quirky schemes.

So here in this merry band,
A salad bowl took a stand.
"Put me in the mix," it cried,
"Let's blend our hopes and joy with pride!"

The Weight of Intention

A ladle heavy with good cheer,
Weighs down thoughts that disappear.
With spices dancing in its grip,
It's ready for the flavor trip.

A frying pan with dreams so bright,
Flips the future, left and right.
It often burns the midnight oil,
Pairing laughter with the toil.

A tiny cup filled to the brim,
With wishes floating, looking slim.
Yet every sip makes laughter bloom,
In a world that's far from gloom.

So here we stack our hopes like plates,
Contented with the funny fates.
And in the chaos, we will bake,
A recipe for joy's sweet sake!

Silent Shapes of Love

In the cupboard, shadows tease,
As mugs whisper, "Let's just freeze!"
Funnels giggle, hiding shy,
While lids roll their eyes, oh my!

An apron folds with secrets grand,
Spilling ketchup, making plans.
A spatula, oh what a tease,
Flips the lovers' hearts with ease.

Silence winks in every nook,
As forks and knives create a hook.
They sketch out dreams with tiny sparks,
While trays dance in the kitchen parks.

A pot's lid clatters, joyfully loud,
As if to say, "Hey, look, I'm proud!"
Together they'll break bread and pie,
And chuckle at the passersby!

Clay Hearts

In a studio where laughter molds,
Sat a quirk with plans to hold.
Embarking on a journey bright,
On wheels that spin with pure delight.

With hands so messy, hearts so bold,
They shape their dreams, or so they told.
A potter's wheel that keeps on twirling,
With jokes and jests, the laughter swirling.

Fired by spirits, glowing red,
Clay figures dance around, they said.
Each bump and groove tells a tale,
Of mishaps that would dare prevail.

So here's to hearts, both soft and tough,
In a world where fun is never rough.
With every twist and every turn,
In the kiln of joy, we always learn!

The Alchemy of Touch

In a kitchen full of quirks,
Laughter dances, then it smirks.
Mixing bits of wrong and right,
Baking joy, what a delight!

A pinch of hope, a dash of cheer,
Stirring up some friendly fear.
With every stir and playful jest,
We shape the world, we do our best.

Like dough that rises, stretched and pulled,
With silly shapes, our hearts are lulled.
In every mess, a story thrives,
In every knot, our laughter dives.

So grab that spoon and hold it tight,
We'll craft our dreams from morning light.
For in this kitchen, bold and bright,
We bake our love with all our might.

Heartstrings in Terracotta

Handmade trinkets, wobbly art,
Each a whisper, from the heart.
Cracked and cherished, they do sing,
Of all the joy that making brings.

With every curve and every line,
We find the truth in silly vine.
Holding tight to what we make,
In pots of laughter, bonds awake.

Firing tales in the warm sun,
Jesting jokes, oh what a fun!
With every laugh and silly slip,
We mold our dreams in every trip.

In pairs of clays, our stories blend,
An orchestra where hearts can mend.
So come, let's shape our silly fate,
In terracotta dreams, we've found our mate.

Shadows of the Wheel

Round and round, the wheel does spin,
As we make shapes, our grins begin.
With every flop, a chuckle swells,
In this dance, our laughter dwells.

Clay flings high, and slips do fly,
Careful now, or pots may sigh.
Hilarity notes in every slip,
Creating chaos in every trip.

So gather close, unleash the fun,
In this bumbling, never-done.
With silly shadows on the wall,
We craft our dreams, and have a ball.

On wheels of clay, we share our hearts,
In messy art, where laughter starts.
Together spinning, we will find,
The rhythm of our lovely bind.

A Recipe for Belonging

A dash of trust and giggles bold,
Stirred with warmth, never cold.
Mix in some quirks, a sprinkle of glee,
A banquet of hearts, you and me.

Gather round, the table set,
With tales of mishaps we won't forget.
Each flavor tells a funny tale,
In this feast, we shall prevail.

Cooked with patience, a dash of spice,
In every bite, there's room for nice.
With every nibble, we grow strong,
In this recipe, we all belong.

So raise a glass to that fine blend,
Where laughter starts and never ends.
For in this kitchen, far and wide,
We find our joy, and side by side.

A Dance of Hands

In a kitchen, all a-jumble,
Flour flies and pots do tumble,
Didn't mean to make a mess,
What a sight, oh what a dress!

Stirring soup and tripping too,
Dance with spoons and break a few,
Laughter echoes, what a sound,
In this chaos, joy is found!

Whisking eggs with playful flair,
A spatula launches in mid-air,
Recipe's lost, but who does care?
Cooking's fun—it's all a dare!

In this whirlwind, smiles switch places,
Sticky fingers, joyful faces,
When we cook, we find delight,
A waltz of hands, a silly sight.

Surrendered to the Fire

Fire flickers, flames do flirt,
Chicken sizzles, jumps and spurt,
"Oh no!" I cry, my hope does waft,
Dinner's dancing, but I've lost craft!

Smoke alarms sing their loud refrain,
What's for dinner? More champagne!
I gallivant, a chef gone wild,
Cooking art or chaos styled?

Let's roast marshmallows, make some treats,
Forget the meat, sweet tooth repeats,
Chocolate drips, oh what a goo,
Surrendered here, to laughter, too.

In the flicker, joy ignites,
Every failure sparks delights,
So grab your forks, let's have a cheer,
A fire dance? Yes, bring it near!

Crafted Dreams

Clay in hands, a little spin,
Mold it tall, yes, let's begin,
A cup? A vase? Oh, what a sight,
Wobbling wonders, oh what a fright!

Turn the wheel, hands barely cling,
Sculptor's art; it's quite the fling,
"Am I making a pot or a frog?"
I need an artsy catalog!

Lopsided bowls and crooked jars,
Future parties? Bring on the stars!
Every layer tells a tale,
Laughter usually won't fail!

In the kiln, my wonders bake,
A masterpiece... or a mistake?
Either way, I'll toast and beam,
For every try was worth a dream!

Unbroken Circles

Gather round, a circle made,
Friends and snacks, a grand parade,
We toss the chips but catch the laughs,
Unbroken circles and silly gaffes.

From passing bowls to stealthy dips,
Watch out for double-dipping slips,
Game night fun, let's joke a bit,
Caught in chaos, we won't quit!

Round and round, our tales unwind,
With every bite, new jests aligned,
Chortles shared in friendly haste,
Every moment, love embraced.

So raise your glass, let's make a pact,
To twist and turn, that's a fact,
In unbroken circles, we find cheer,
Funny lives shared, bringing us near!

Transient Touch

In the corner sat a mug,
A chip where I poured my love.
It wobbled, danced, then took a fall,
Said, "Oops! I meant to win it all."

A teapot dreamed of fancy tea,
But had a lid that wouldn't flee.
"More pour, less spill, that's my request!"
Yet every brew became a jest.

The kettle whistled loud and clear,
A sound that made the cat appear.
With one quick leap, oh what a mess,
Now shards of clay and feline stress.

So here's to clay in all its forms,
With quirks and giggles through the storms.
We raise a cup to every crack,
Each laugh a memory, no looking back.

Time Woven in Earthenware

In the cupboard sits a plate,
Once held a feast, now holds debate.
"Am I a charger or a dish?"
It dreams of meals and a fine swish.

A bowl that swayed with every dip,
Said, "Chili, soup, or just a quip?"
It held mischief on its rim,
And laughed at toppings, lost and grim.

The glasses clank with all their might,
While keeping secrets through the night.
One cracked a joke, a laugh erupted,
Now all of them seem slightly corrupted.

Through time, the clay does shift and mold,
Each piece a story waiting to be told.
Let's raise our voices, let them chatter,
In the dance of life, what truly matters?

Tenderly Forged

In the workshop, sparks flew bright,
Molded dreams took to flight.
"I'm a cup, not just a shell!"
It blushed and rang like a jolly bell.

Out on shelves, the vases grin,
Holding flowers, feeling kin.
"Look at me! I've got great style!"
One pointed to the past, all the while.

A saucer sighed with vintage grace,
"Can't we travel from this place?"
While collecting dust, it raised a cheer,
"At least I'm clean, not stuck in beer!"

These creations sing with all their flaws,
In every dent, there's applause.
Crafted with laughter, not with strife,
They hold the quirks that color life.

In the Hearth's Glow

By the fire, the kettle danced,
With a wobbly jig, it pranced.
"Come on, tea! Don't lose your speed!"
One brown spot turned to a novel breed.

Plates were piled with floppy fries,
Salads served with little lies.
"Who knew greens could make you sick?"
They sent out vibes both fresh and thick.

Mugs held tales of morning woe,
With coffee stains forming a bow.
"Am I more than just a sipper?"
Echoed through each daily dripper.

Around the hearth, each piece did glow,
Crafted with stories only we know.
Raise a glass to tremors of mirth,
In every crack, there's fun on Earth.

The Clay That Binds

In the studio, we twist and twirl,
Molding mischief, watch it swirl.
Lopsided bowls and wonky cups,
A masterpiece? You must be nuts!

Glazing dreams in colors bright,
Crafting chaos, what a sight!
Our hands are messy, but who will care?
A pot to hold our dreams laid bare.

Fired up with laughter, it's all a game,
Each crack and chip, a badge of fame.
With every wobble, we all agree,
This won't win the pottery spree!

So here's to our clay, our jolly mess,
Each pot a story, more or less.
While critics frown and clasp their jaws,
We'll sip from cups with funny flaws!

Spheres of Ambition

Rolling marbles of bright design,
We dream of trophies, oh so fine.
But here they sit, each painted sphere,
An avocado, what a cheer!

Chasing dreams with playful spins,
A glob of clay, where laughter begins.
Round and round the ambitions roll,
Plus one more for that pizza goal!

With every turn, we pull a face,
The perfect art? Not in this place.
Giggles echo as we misalign,
Yet every mess is simply divine!

So toast to spheres and wobbly dreams,
Full of laughter and silly schemes.
For in our hearts, they all will shine,
Brightly colored, a grand design!

Garden of Whispers

In a garden of clay, we plant our cheer,
With pots that wobble and jokes we hear.
A gnome that giggles, a sunflower bright,
We'll laugh 'til dusk, what a sight!

Each flower a friend, each pot a tale,
With daisies dancing, we'll set sail.
A zucchini named Bob, asks for a sip,
Of lemonade made from a clayey drip!

Whispers of laughter float in the air,
As we share secrets with overgrown hair.
Even the weeds have taken a stand,
Making a mess in our improvised land!

So here in this garden, friendships bloom,
With funny critters and everyday gloom.
Let's raise our pots and have a toast,
To the joys of clay, we love the most!

Vows in Clay

In a chic little shop, we exchange our vows,
With cups made crooked, we raise our brows.
A sculpture of hope, but wait - it's a fish,
Winked at by laughter, what a funny dish!

We promise to cherish, until it unglues,
Each vase a memory, a colorful ruse.
When it cracks, we will giggle and cheer,
For each silly piece tells a tale sincere!

So here's to the laughter, the joy we create,
With each funny pot, our dreams resonate.
In every mishap, our hearts intertwine,
With clay as our witness, love's pure design!

In the end, our craft is a messy delight,
We'll spin tales of joy, morning to night.
With vows in our hearts and clay on our hands,
Together we'll build our whimsical lands!

A Symphony of Clay

In a studio bright, clay spins round,
Laughter erupts with each silly sound.
With splashes of mud, we dance and we twirl,
Creating a monster, a weird little whirl.

Our hands all a-glue, we sculpt with delight,
A frog wearing glasses, a comical sight.
"Is that really a mug?" our friend starts to ask,
"Or a vase with a frog in a whimsical mask?"

When the kiln roars to life, we all hold our breath,
Will it crack, will it break, or bring life after death?
A treasure or trash, we await with a grin,
For in every misstep, new laughter begins.

So let's shape our dreams with a giggle or two,
For art's not perfection, it's joy, wouldn't you?
Let the clay tell its tales, all the blunders we make,
In this zany adventure, we've nothing to break.

Molding Trust

With squishy hands and a grin so wide,
We mold our visions, with giggles, we slide.
"Is it a bowl or a hat?" we all cheer,
As mud flies around, bringing joy, bringing cheer.

Crafting connections, no smooth path in sight,
Through jigs and through jags, we find sheer delight.
"In every wobble, there's laughter," we say,
As our 'masterpieces' start to sway and play.

When the wheel spins fast, oh, what a scene,
A sculpture of chaos, a mishmash so keen.
"Look, it's a monster that wants a snack!"
We chuckle together, "Let's give it a whack!"

With each playful fail, we nod and we grin,
In this messy old art, we just can't forget.
So loosen your grip, let the clay take its hold,
For each blunder we make is a story retold.

The Fragments of Faith

In pieces we gather, our humor a spark,
We fuse all the bits in a light-hearted lark.
"Is that part of a vase or some odd architecture?"
We cackle and snort, our laughter the best feature.

With shards all around, oh, what will we do?
We stick them together, it's a chaotically gluey zoo.
"What happened here?" our curator might scream,
"It's avant-garde art, or that's just our theme!"

Each crack tells a joke, each groove has a tale,
Our faith in the clay continues to prevail.
In every misfit, we see our own grace,
Creating a masterpiece with a laugh on its face.

So flutter those fingers, let the magic commence,
For in bits and in chunks is our joy, immense.
With every odd shape, we celebrate cheer,
In this happily fractured mosaic, we steer.

Echoes from the Kiln

We gather around as the kiln starts to hum,
With hopes held high for our crafts to come.
"Will it be splendid or a total disaster?
Let's wait and see—what will come faster?"

The timer ticks down, we exchange silly grins,
Will our art be a triumph, or crumbled with sins?
A loud crack echoes, our hearts jump with fright,
"Did someone's creation just take a hard bite?"

When the door swings open, we all rush to peek,
A rainbow of colors! It's a colorful freak!
"Turns out my jug's a peculiar pink shoe,"
We laugh at our blunders, as friendships break through.

So let's shout our cheers for the quirky and wild,
For in every odd artifact, there's joy compiled.
With clinking of mugs, we'll toast to the clay,
In this playful chaos, we'll happily stay.

A Tapestry of Earth

In the garden, mud was king,
With laughter loud, and worms that sing.
We crafted dreams in crooked shapes,
And giggled at our silly fates.

The daisies danced, they knew our play,
While insects joined in disarray.
We built our castles, tall and round,
Then watched them tumble to the ground.

From clumps of clay and laughter free,
We fashioned art, a sight to see.
A masterpiece of blunders bright,
Embracing chaos, pure delight.

So here's to splashes, bright and bold,
And stories from our hands, retold.
We'll cherish moments, messy and sweet,
In the tapestry of our lighthearted feat.

Whispers from the Studio

In the studio, what's that sound?
The pots are laughing all around.
With quirky shapes and colors wild,
They tease the artist, oh so riled!

A mug with ears, a bowl that sings,
Refusing to follow common things.
With each turn of the crafting wheel,
Our funny dreams begin to heal.

Clay squished here, and clay squished there,
We mold our hopes with playful flair.
Silly faces on plates so round,
Becoming art we're proud to sound.

Laughter echoes as we create,
In the studio, we celebrate.
Our quirky touches, alight with glee,
In this wacky world we call 'the spree.'

Strength in the Structure

Building dreams with arms out wide,
We stack our hopes, no need to hide.
With bricks of giggles and mortar fun,
Our silly structures have begun.

The walls may wobble, the roof may sway,
But who needs straight lines in play?
With every whim, we add a twist,
In this crazy game, we can't resist.

A tower here, a wobbly stair,
Uneven ground? Oh, we don't care!
For every laugh, a brick we lay,
In this delightful blue-sky ballet.

So let's embrace the funky build,
Where frights of form are gently stilled.
In laughter, we find our perfect ground,
In this structure of joy, we're tightly bound.

Fields of Handprints

In fields of color, fingers gleam,
We leave our marks, like in a dream.
With splatters bright, we paint the air,
Handprints dancing everywhere!

The grass a canvas, wide and free,
We stomp and laugh, wild as can be.
Each print a tale, a giggle shared,
In these fields, no one is scared.

With every hue, our spirits rise,
Like sunlit laughter in the skies.
Imprints of joy, they tell our story,
Playing in colors, in all their glory.

So let's be messy, joyous and bold,
In fields of handprints, warmth unfolds.
A celebration of friendship true,
In every splash, a vibrant hue.

Echoes of the Intentional

In the cupboard, things collide,
A dish that spins and runs to hide.
I swear it dances in the night,
Laughing softly, what a sight!

Forks and spoons conspire too,
To create a culinary coup.
With a wink, they make a toast,
To their friends, they love the most.

Cups that giggle, bowls that grin,
All seem ready for a win.
Chopsticks practice their ballet,
In a kitchen cabaret, hooray!

With each clink, a story told,
Of bonds that thrive, yet never fold.
So here's to laughter, merriment wide,
In circles where our treasures reside.

Bound by Art

A canvas painted with a laugh,
Brushes dance, a joyful path.
Colors splatter, joy ignites,
Creating chaos, pure delights.

Hang the frames upon the walls,
Echoing sketches, art that calls.
Each stroke tells a funny tale,
Of mishaps that will never fail.

Glues and pastes in wild debate,
As glitter tries to dominate.
Crayons rival with their flair,
In the gallery of despair!

But here we bond, in hues so bright,
Crafting laughter, pure delight.
For where there's mess, there's love in art,
Connected close, we play our part.

The Texture of Trust

In a kitchen crafted from delight,
Feeling secrets rise to height.
A rolling pin, a sassy twirl,
Whispers of dough in a playful whirl.

Kneading laughter into bread,
With every punch, our fears shed.
A pinch of salt, a dash of cheer,
Trust gets baked, unique, my dear!

Ovens hum a friendly tune,
While spatulas dance beneath the moon.
Baking's a sport, or so they say,
With each misfire, a new cliché!

Let's frolic in flour, bound by fate,
Telling stories that can't be late.
For in the heat, we learn and try,
Together we rise, oh my, oh my!

Shapes of Tomorrow

With cookie cutters, we make dreams,
Surprising shapes, or so it seems.
A crescent moon or star so bright,
Imperfect forms, yet pure delight.

Flour dusted dreams take flight,
In a world where wrong feels right.
Edible futures, rolled in dough,
Who knew tomorrow could taste so slow?

Spoons of fate stir heartfelt tales,
Creating magic in wild gales.
Each cookie's shape, a plot divine,
To shape a world, together we dine.

So here's to confections, sweet and grand,
Designing tomorrows, hand in hand.
Let's bake our laughter, rise with glee,
For here's a future, just you and me!

Vessels of Hope

A bowl once dreamt of being a hat,
But fell on the floor with a splat.
Its friends all laughed, what a great feat,
Now it's a home for some old parakeet.

A mug with a crack wanted to sing,
But all it could do was sway in the spring.
With tea it was filled, then promptly forgot,
Now it just sits, in a dusty old spot.

A jug wished for grandeur, a life full of cheers,
But it spends every night drowning in beers.
With laughter it's filled, with hope it is drained,
A life like a party, that's uncontained!

Yet each vessel's charm brings a chuckle or two,
Their stories are silly; oh, what can they do?
In colors they glimmer, each shape holds a whim,
For life's a grand joke and they're all in on him!

Secrets in the Slip

A little pot sighed, with a glaze that was shy,
It wanted to sparkle, but oh my, oh my!
Each swirl on its back told a tale of its plight,
Yet the kiln's heat was a bit too polite.

A teapot once peeked from the edge of a shelf,
Wishing for tea parties, but just served itself.
With a grin on its face, it poured out its foe,
A bubble-filled brew that was all froth and no flow!

A saucer once dreamed of a dance at the ball,
But ended up stuck with a plate, that's all.
They swayed in the cupboard, what a sight to behold,
Two mismatched maidens, brimming with gold!

With each clink and clatter, secrets only they know,
About lives in the cupboard, a whimsical show.
In the world of the fragile, humor holds sway,
As they giggle and bicker at the end of the day!

The Gesture of Forming

A lump of clay wished for a twist,
To dance on a wheel, oh what bliss!
With a spin here and a poke there,
It turned into a thing that forgot to declare.

A vase tried to blossom, a garden it dreamed,
But the flowers inside just wilted and steamed.
With water it filled, and hope it contained,
Yet the secret it held was slightly drained.

A sculpture of bronze asked for some flair,
To dance through the night, with style and care.
But all it could do was wobble and rock,
An art piece they mocked, a wobbly block!

With each poke and prod, there's magic and jest,
As shapes come to life, but fail the behest.
For in the world of modeling, laughter ensures,
That every odd shape is a treasure that purrs!

Lifetimes in the Clay

Once a humble piece in the mud, it lay low,
Dreaming of grand things, like a potpourri show.
With each twist and turn, it finally took shape,
But soon it was shocked to find itself drape!

A jug with a handle, it tried to reminisce,
Of birthdays long past, with a tinge of bliss.
But during the party, it spilled all the cake,
Now it's known more for the mess than the flake!

An ashtray admired all the folks passing by,
It held all their secrets, oh my, oh my!
Yet each little puff was sometimes a chore,
It held onto dreams, like a porcelain bore!

Through mishaps and dreams, in the stage of display,
These fractured old vessels just laugh at the fray.
For in every crack lies a tale full of cheer,
In the world of the silly, we all hold them dear!

Glazed Intentions

In a shop of clay and charm,
I tried to fix that broken arm.
With duct tape and a silly grin,
I thought, "Now let the fun begin!"

The pot complained with every crack,
"You'll never get this back on track!"
But I just laughed and spilled some glue,
"Let's see what chaos we can do!"

Each dish a story, every mug a tale,
Of mishaps and a wobbly fail.
I promise you, it's all in jest,
Just laugh at life, and do your best!

So here's to pots both big and small,
With each new drip, we'll have a ball!
Raise a toast to this wild dance,
In the land of clay, we take a chance!

Whispered Wishes in Porcelain

A teacup dreams of lofty heights,
While saucers sway on shared delights.
They gossip soft beneath the sun,
About the mishaps, oh so fun!

"I wish to be a sturdy bowl,"
Said one in hopes to take control.
"I'd rather be a plate of fame,
With food to seal my porcelain name!"

The coffee pot just laughed out loud,
"I'd rather brew with all the crowd.
Forget those dreams of grandeur wide,
Let's spill our joys, not hide inside!"

So here they danced, a funny show,
With every wobble, they'd steal the glow.
In a world where clinks and clatters sing,
Cup and plate unite in zing!

Heartbeats in Terracotta

In the garden, pots stand in rows,
With secrets buried 'neath the snows.
One claimed, "I've got a heart of clay,
And I'm just waiting for the day!"

A neighbor whispered, "Don't you fret,
We'll fill you up, and you'll forget!"
With soil piled high and seeds of fun,
Life blooms here, and we all run!

Terracotta dreams of hearty laughs,
Chasing after watering pacts.
Together we'll grow, in sun and rain,
What a crazy, lovely terrain!

So raise your pots, and cheer aloud,
For every mistake, we'll be proud.
In dirt and giggles, we find our place,
With heartbeats shared, life's a race!

Sculpted Aspirations

In the studio, the clay is free,
Rolling shapes of glee and glee!
"I want to be the fanciest vase,
With tulips bright and a shiny face!"

Another shouted, "Not so fast!
I'll make you wobbly, hope you last!"
Fingers dance, a playful fight,
In sculpted dreams, all feels so right.

With every swirl, a laugh ensues,
"What's next?" they giggle, "Shiny hues!"
A bowl responds, "I'd rather spill,
Than stand so proud and lose the thrill!"

So mold those laughs, and sculpt our cheer,
In a world of clay, there's naught to fear.
Our funny shapes will charm the soul,
In crafted hopes, we find our role!

Ceramics of Hope

In a shop of quirky wares,
A cup with legs and funny stares.
It wobbles when I take my sip,
But still, it's got a funny grip.

A teapot shaped like a cat,
That purrs when filled, imagine that!
It spills tea with a playful cheer,
While I just laugh and sip my beer.

A bowl that dances on the shelf,
It thinks it's quite the acrobat elf.
But when I pour in cereal sweet,
It leaps and tumbles, what a feat!

With every piece, a chuckle grows,
Life's too short for boring shows.
So here's to laughter in each glaze,
In this quirky world, I'll stay amazed.

Vessels of Vow

A vase that sways like a ballerina,
Filled with flowers and a tease of hyena.
It whispers secrets of scent and cheer,
And sometimes tips, oh dear, oh dear!

A jug that jigs with a belly so round,
When filled, it booms a silly sound.
Promises bubble in frothy delight,
While I dance with joy, oh what a sight!

A plate that tells of pies in the sun,
But rolls away when dinner's begun.
With every meal, it makes a dash,
Away from veggies, oh what a clash!

We laugh at these vessels, full of quirks,
In this canvas of clay, just silly perks.
So raise a toast with a grinning cup,
To these funny friends that lift us up.

Clay Dreams Unfurled

In the land where clay is king,
Mugs dance and sing, oh what a fling!
A bowl that giggles when filled with soup,
Turns into a playful, splashing loop!

A quirky butter dish with wobbly feet,
Slides off the table, oh what a feat!
It lands with a splat, so funny and loud,
While we all cheer, feeling so proud.

A teacup with eyes that blink in surprise,
In every sip, there's laughter that flies.
It spills tea in fits, a bubbly exclaim,
Keeping our spirits ever aflame.

Our little dreams made from soft, squishy clay,
Bring joy and giggles throughout the day.
So let's gather round, let's raise cheer,
For these silly creations that bring us near.

The Earthen Oath

A platter that swears it can serve dessert,
But oftentimes ends up muddy and hurt.
With every cake it claims to host,
It's more of a comical, clay-coated boast!

A cup that claims to hold the best brew,
But tips over often, just like a shoe.
It giggles each time it spills on the floor,
And we can't help but laugh more and more.

A pitcher that vows to pour without fuss,
But dribbles and runs, what a ruckus!
With every gulp, we find some more,
Of laughter, spills, and slippery floor.

So here's to the clay that captures each joke,
Each funny moment, each heartfelt poke.
With earthen creations, our lives remain bright,
In a world full of whimsy and pure delight.

A Memory in the Mud

In the garden, a treasure lies,
Buried deep, a prize in disguise.
Old boots with blooms, oh what a sight,
A muddy marvel, pure delight.

Trowels and laughter, a daily chore,
Each shovel reveals tales of yore.
Giggling worms, a wriggly crew,
Together we dig, and joke anew.

Mischief sprouted, like weeds in spring,
A muddy disaster, oh what a fling!
Giant shoes splashed, laughter's pure sound,
In the muck, our joys abound.

So here's to the dirt, where memories play,
In the muck, we dance, without delay.
A garden of giggles, our hearts all entwined,
In the mud, our humor defined.

Reveries in Porcelain

In a china shop, where dreams take flight,
Cups dance and spin, oh what a sight!
Tea parties brewed, with giggles galore,
Every sip sparks joy, forever more.

A saucer slips with a comedic clatter,
Chinaware chuckles, what's the matter?
Teacups gossip like friends in a huddle,
While saucers roll in a playful muddle.

With each delicate piece, a tale is spun,
Of dashing teapots and mischief begun.
Laughter rings out in a porcelain spree,
Where memories and fun spill like tea.

So let's toast to the clumsy, the joyful, the cheer,
In the world of fine china, we hold dear.
For laughter and love, in each little crack,
Makes a lovely reminder, we'll never look back.

The Shape of Affection

In a world made round, with hugs and smiles,
Hearts overlapping, stretching for miles.
We bake sweet circles, pies for the crew,
With love in each slice, and laughter so true.

A square box holds treasures, knickknacks of cheer,
With quirky surprises that bring you near.
Rectangles of hopes, like pancakes askew,
Flipping our dreams, a breakfast debut.

Oh, the shapes of affection swirl all around,
In each silly gesture, joy is found.
From hearts to handshakes, the forms intermixed,
Creating a tapestry, we'd never fix.

So let's revel in shapes, so fun and divine,
From circles to squares, our hearts intertwine.
For in every contour, in every design,
We shape our affection, one laugh at a time.

Formed in Trust

A pot once cracked, held secrets so dear,
Two friends had a pact, to always stay near.
With every chip, a tale to express,
In laughter, we forged a delightful mess.

Glue and paint, a patchwork delight,
Restored with humor, shining so bright.
Each repair a giggle, each flaw a jest,
In the art of mending, we find our best.

Trust is the clay, molded with care,
A vessel of humor, for all to share.
In every mishap, in every repair,
We laugh with abandon, breathing sweet air.

So here's to the bonds, both funny and true,
In cracked little pots, our friendship grew.
For in every flaw, a story to share,
We are formed in trust, in laughter and care.

Language of the Hands

Fingers dance like butterflies,
Creating tales with every sigh.
A point here, a wave over there,
Their stories float upon the air.

Grabbing air, a wild charade,
The thumbs up, an awkward parade.
Waving hello, then tripping on floor,
Life's funny, oh, how we adore!

Scribbles in the air, a secret code,
Helping us speak, lighten the load.
A gesture slips, oh, what a thrill,
The hands just whisper, but left us ill!

In this charmed dance, we talk and preen,
With laughs and chuckles, hearts so keen.
A clumsy touch or a missed high-five,
In this banter, our spirits thrive!

Tender Clay and Truth

Molding truths with silly grins,
Laughter erupts when clay begins.
A shape that's odd or a wiggle here,
What was a vase is now a deer!

Hands get messy, oh what luck,
An art disaster, full of muck.
A snicker here, a giggle there,
The truth in clay is rare and fair.

Forming dreams, we twist and spin,
Rounding edges just to win.
With every squish and every poke,
A life of fun, not just a joke!

In this bright light, we take our stand,
Crafting joy with a giggling hand.
So here's to clay, let spirits soar,
In this silly mess, who could want more?

Hopes Baked at Dawn

A sprinkle here, a dash of cheer,
Gooey dough brings laughter near.
The oven hums, it's almost done,
A morning bake, oh, what a fun!

Round the table, a mishap's found,
The muffins rise with a funny sound.
The timer beeps, the chaos grows,
A burnt batch? Well, everyone knows!

Sweet smells waft through the morning light,
Hopes rise, but so do the slight bites.
Flavors mix in a jolly dance,
In this storm, we laugh and prance!

With coffee sipped and crumbs in hand,
We toast to chaos, it's truly grand.
Who needs perfection? We just want fun,
With hopes baked warmly, let's eat and run!

Cracks that Speak

In every chip, a tale unfolds,
Of laughter shared and secrets told.
A crack in the vase, oh what a jest,
It's a badge of honor, not a pest!

Listen closely, the lines will chat,
Unfolding stories, oh what's that?
A patchwork voiced through time and cheer,
Life's little bites that bring us near.

Wobbly shapes have their own beat,
With quirks and quirks, they're quite the treat!
A mug that winks, a plate that sighs,
They hold our laughter, not just ties.

So here's to cracks, our quirkiest kind,
In their embraces, warmth we find.
Let's toast to flaws, to loopy fun,
In every chip, life's finest spun!

Grounded in Love

In the kitchen, chaos reigns,
Silly dances through the stains.
Baking bread with a wobble and sway,
Who knew dough could lead us astray?

Egg on face, flour in hair,
Laughter bursts, we're a wild pair.
Mixing joy like it's a game,
With a dash of sugar and a splash of fame.

Whisking dreams, we take a chance,
Stirring hope in a funny dance.
Even if we drop the mix,
We'll laugh it off, these little tricks.

Each little spill, a tale to weave,
In a world of whimsy, we believe.
Love simmering in a pot of cheer,
Together always, never fear.

Embrace the Impermanent

A vase today, tomorrow a frown,
Easily toppled, as we tumble down.
Laughing at cracks, we make them art,
Each little chip, a punchline to start.

We juggle feelings, a bumpy ride,
Like a clown car, full of pride.
Nothing's fixed, it's all a show,
Embrace the quirks, let them flow.

The teacups dance, they play a joke,
One tips over, and then they poke.
Drink your tea with a side of glee,
Life's too funny to take seriously.

So here's to the slips and falls we make,
In our funny hats, let's celebrate!
For in the wobbles of our fate,
We find the joy we cultivate.

Through the Artist's Eyes

Brushes dance, colors collide,
Splashes and strokes, nothing to hide.
Each muddled hue tells a tale,
We giggle at art, oh what a scale!

A cupcake depicted in vibrant swirls,
Melting icing, oh how it twirls.
Can you taste this whimsical feast?
Art in laughter, never a beast.

We sculpt strange shapes, with flair and fun,
A snickering monster might just run!
Laughter rings as clay squishes tight,
Making silliness through the night.

In the gallery of our delight,
Where nothing is wrong, everything's right.
Creating joy, with humor and cheer,
An artist's eye brings the world near.

A Tapestry of Touch

Threads of laughter, stitch by stitch,
In a world where friends can switch.
Gathered round, we weave the tale,
With stories bright and colors pale.

A knot of kindness, snug and tight,
Tickled by joy in the morning light.
Snip the worries, toss them aside,
In this merry quilt, we take pride.

Fabric of friendship, rough and smooth,
Life's patchwork gifts, we all approve.
Each quirky patch tells a tale,
With stitches that giggle and never pale.

In this tapestry, our hearts align,
Woven with humor, each little line.
Embrace the wild, the soft and loud,
In the fabric of life, we're joyfully proud.

The Silent Covenant of Stoneware

In a cupboard so tight, secrets reside,
Cup and saucer, side by side.
They pledge to never chip or crack,
While hiding snacks behind their back.

A plate dreams of pasta, steaming hot,
While a bowl contemplates a lonely spot.
Together they laugh, beneath the light,
In a dance of dust, out of sight.

They giggle in glazes, all shiny and bright,
Echoes of dinners, a whimsical night.
When saucy adventures and crumbs abound,
These silent vessels, joyfully sound.

So clink your mugs, let the laughter flow,
In a cupboard full of memories aglow.
For though they won't shout, their bond is clear,
These stoneware friends hold stories dear.

Bowls of Belief

Once a bowl claimed it could hold the whole moon,
In a world where gravity's quite opportune.
With a wink and a nod, they all believed,
But oh dear bowl, were you misperceived?

Another said, "I'm an ocean vast!"
Yet in reality, she wasn't built to last.
With cereal inside, she took a brave stance,
And wobbled away, avoiding the chance.

In the face of chips, their confidence shone,
Declaring, "We're fine, we'll never be alone!"
For every scrape holds a tale, it's true,
In kitchens with giggles, sharing the view.

Together they clash, a whirlpool of cheer,
With soups and spaghetti, their mission is clear.
Bowls of belief in a world vast and wide,
Spinning their hopes with scrapes thrown aside.

Fired Futures

In the kiln of existence, dreams get baked,
A daring adventure, none can forsake.
With ash on their cheeks, they pop and cheer,
Planning escapes, their futures seem near.

A mug dreams of coffee, hot and robust,
While a tiny teacup swirls in its trust.
Together they plot, with humor in tow,
Imagining virtues in a teapot's glow.

Mismatched and chipped, they're still full of zing,
Trading hot gossip like a well-tuned string.
"Oh, the things we might be!" they giggle and sway,
As the whirlwind of clay shapes a bright, funny day.

And although they may crack, through thick and thin,
They toast with a cheer—'Let the fun begin!'
In the fired futures of clay's sweet embrace,
They dance on the shelf, a whimsical place.

Unbroken Craft

In a workshop bustling, where laughter does bloom,
A family of mugs raise their cheer in the room.
"Raise your handles high!" they joyfully sing,
Crafted together, let's see what we bring.

With paints and with glaze, all quirky and bright,
They tease each other, each daring delight.
"I'm the best!" grumbles a worn-out old cup,
But a gentle new saucer says, "Hey, fill up!"

For every mishap, a giggle it brings,
In the spirit of art, the imagination sings.
As clay flies around in a rhythmic old dance,
They bust out their dreams, giving fate a chance.

Unbroken in spirit, they stand side by side,
Through mishaps and laughter, they take it in stride.
From pots made of clay, to treasures so bold,
Their crafted communion is a joy to behold.

www.ingramcontent.com/pod-product-compliance
Lightning Source LLC
Chambersburg PA
CBHW070309120526
44590CB00017B/2605